I0224789

Beyond That Hill I Gather

poems by

Jeffrey Kingman

Finishing Line Press
Georgetown, Kentucky

Beyond That Hill I Gather

ACKNOWLEDGMENTS

"Norma Jeane Mortenson" (a previous version) appeared in *Crack the Spine,* Issue
112, May 7, 2014.

"Ever Listening: Kristin Hersh" (a previous version) was published in Quiet
Lightning's *Sparkle + Blink,* number 63, 2015.

"Sadie" was published in *Picaroon Poetry,* Fall 2016.

"Heidi of the Alps" was published in *The Offbeat,* Spring 2017.

"Clarice Lispector" was published in *Ursa Minor,* Volume 2, 2017.

"'A Posterity Conceived and Born of Conscious Love'" was published on the
Poydras Review blog on August 26, 2019.

"Billie Holiday" was published in *Waving Hands Review,* Issue 11, 2019

"Patti Smith: Lost Objects" "Muriel Spark" and "Joan Rivers" were published in
Visitant, April, May, and June 2020.

Publisher: Leah Huete de Maines
Editor: Christen Kincaid
Cover Art: Katy Miessner
            Clockwise from top left:
            Cherie Currie, Billie Holiday, Melva Kingman, Mary Gawthorpe
Author Photo: Katy Miessner
Cover Design: Krystal Hipps

Order online: www.finishinglinepress.com
            also available on amazon.com

Author inquiries and mail orders:
Finishing Line Press
P. O. Box 1626
Georgetown, Kentucky 40324
U. S. A.

Table of Contents

III.

for Melva

I.

How Did It Make You Feel When They Found You

played tennis with Ted yesterday
he said Dad hasn't written
he sees me different now
   burnt skin that flickers

Dad used to warn us
when we shoved each other down stairs
dance moves furniture by the wayside

I went into pictures
   my sunlight trapped
in the black curl at my cheek
nobody now even sees

I sweep up my bangs
   my forehead gleams
from what I read in Tolstoy
   and Schopenhauer
I've let all that heat escape

before they found me
   I was walking a street
way out
where there was no edge to the expanding city

Matriarch

ninth great-grandchild
spits up peas
seventh and fourth
declare themselves winners

I bundle the children into categories
high shouldered daughters gobble minutes
trikes in the hallway

my sidewinding wisdom
laughs into a hanky

why is it I depend on the perpetual
tweed skirt

try reading
a mother
nursing triplets

attagirl

I suppose getting it right doesn't matter
pull the flowers from the earth

an isolated pea is a tiny thing

Lost Objects: Patti Smith

kitchen shrinks
the mind small framed
pantry quietly slowing
tiny black fish breathe briny
oxygen alive
frying in the pan
sound scratched
lungs aplenty but minute breath
sink drips
sit herself stay herself
smaller sippy
widen water hotter
daughter husband coffee coffee
coffee coffee coffee

small photograph
for the camera
sit behind it
screen door
the picture taker leaving
is he a William or a Fred
I'm dying now he says
but still he saves her
glue holds them
the very stickiness
leaves her herself
at the bungalow
going away saying hello
to dye a red object red

The Way Back Home: Muriel Spark

1.
why and where a tinsel coronet
chosen queen of poetry
so nice to have one's hair stroked by a teacher
she submerges her telephone his words moisten

faraway languages spill from her unheld hand
alone she wanders south africa
what a long walk and with a baby robin to feed

the earth chafes and the baby's beak so sharp
a young woman out lost must test each thorn

she looks down through the parasol trees
wet swooshing incessant spray
leopards are harmless it's the yellow oxalis
chases her home

2.
now it's just front porch azaleas
the sun must have set and the school closed
even the walls evaporating
only voices left
she must form the words dryly

yes her hair was nice
                    the old teacher said

Offspring

Babies are a crisp pile of leaves.
Warm the pile, they soften, dance

without strings
their mother
inside them.

Mothers die young
then work harder.

No, I haven't forgotten.
I roam the stairways and listen

to the tap-tapping of falling marbles.

Josephine Marcus Earp

cowboys were the bad guys
    one cow hides behind the last one
it was a bad sum
    inaccuracies plus chickens

instead traded on horse hooves
kicked up dust and stray dogs

she wanted to be
    taken seriously
staked instead a vagabond

her husband's posture straight to the sky
    pointing now to the headboard
the tombstone didn't think of her

left with her own version
they rifle through the undergarment drawer
    for the sheriff's girl

Clarice Lispector

Brazilians ask, How was Hell?
Hell dreamt me and I came to life speaking jaguarundese.

I was from there, now I'm from here.
The pink so tall it never ends, a forest.
Pernambuco dialect of fruit sellers. I see it
more clearly now … my childhood house, the bridge, the river.
There is a future beyond the body, while the past
is of blood. Everything is between these two sleeps.

With a bag of confetti and a crepe paper dress
Father sent me to the pharmacy on an urgent errand.
Carnival revelers twitched and ticked.
When I returned, at the window she still hadn't moved.
But she never did. My dad used to move her.
Mother was killed by Ukrainian semen but
died in Brazil where I'd already named
each tile in the bathroom.

Yes, Jews were thrown from trains. I know.
I am Brazilian.
To escape on a vile boat is a puny miracle. It allowed Father to peddle
in northern Brazil where there was nothing but a port.
But I was happy catching mice and stealing roses
the thrill as I broke the stems.
Colors don't end
they vanish into the air.

In Ukraine they say, "Tell us, Clarice."
But I won't. I say something else.

Help Me Out Can You: Elizabeth Holloway Marston

9:00am appointment re the mammal article
editing staff meeting
lunch with Sanger
hold all calls except re baby
                      temperature

experiment with pins
have four hands
husband barks about the noise
                    has no office

first her household
          then the work
what is done with a baby
                or two
is done to reduce options

green crayon
         notes under doors
boy wants to be a mom
               kids are reporters
there aren't many ways to diaper
                     apparent
what is this woman doing

Cherie Currie

innocent about schoolwork
about goatees and doubt
about homesick smog
and gagging
giggles the stifling hours
wants younger and prettier
just Dorothy spins
before landing shuffled fears
down the street
the fever
the pansy-ass
the purple garage dirty trailer
the bastard cocksucker tapping along
the nine or ten younger and
prettier in the Glasgow dark

Marie a tight laugh
holding back a hug
gagging and coughing
was in the hate
Mr. Rosencrantz goateed and tan
smiling and nodding OK alright
Lita: fuck yeah fuck yeah
taught Woolite hotel miss
you so much into words
you should be jogging
PS hope you like my
little gift Japan they get us
not just Bali Monkees
                    Mom said

back home
Cheap Trick opened
my Aunt Evie
Dad everyone
prime entertainment Joan
slung pacing

purple's smiling cool-fuck
shuffled fears thinking
the thoughtful congratulatory
dogs ruin it at nine or ten
make-or-break a little about
                    money

Garbo/Dietrich

how my sister and I made-believe we were
    boys playing rough
yes I burn ticks squash spiders
you must've compared notes

you spoke out loud everyone
    could hear
your trail of bees
I listen
    your voice was the phonograph

my unpainted lips are the burgundy
    you expect yours to be
I fling up handfuls of primrose
    and you shrug

go ahead
shock them with your pants and necktie
pretend we never met

clasp my unconscious body
support me firmly under my arm
    with your right hand

your left hand on my shoulder
    as I slip to the ground
we should've rehearsed

Sure: Mother Maybelle

I heard you
          rattling enormous pans
chopping parsnips and beef.
Says you are Celebrity
and that you pick
both parts.
But you're not sure.
You swim beside your ducklings.

I heard you
          playing your guitar.

H.D., the Book

You are a book now.
The author understands his work.
  I plough through words
  scatter you on either side.

II.

Covered

a simple question
dropped into a hole
wearing a headscarf

carries a burden
born of failing
to listen

a vase is broken
or a girl pregnant
a book lip balm water in the fountain

the hole gets wider
the scarf wrapped tighter
strike the words (a leading answer)

explain over tea at their doorsteps
kids disappear from the streets
tell the driver keep going
there and there

is she this woman
contain her mosaic identity
in the water
puff the water pipe
become unstuck

like black lashes
on a sink

it covers her
purple fabric brilliant
all is smoothed over
get paid for breast-feeding

Demonstration

Spatula—an object comfort
of doing

philosophize roasting
flesh drip aura

of food simmering
stockyards, factories.

Insert cosmetic flowers in suckling
eye sockets.

Watch for delivery—by what mode
at the waxed floor.

Carton of pigs lifted.
Rounded biceps grunt

oxcart, truck, ship, cargo plane
turtle beans

and wine unloaded
into the towering kitchen.

Build   Devour   Digest
great empires

in solitude   reflect.

Provocative statements
such as this one: "If we were to

(What can be stated in a cookbook.)

Bergamot, limes
by ship, mallow of marsh.

Althaea officinalis
Julia Child remote

delicate herb
black and white oven.

Leaving Home, 1959

1.
No, cotton wouldn't bother me there
though I fingered it nervously.
Jan dropped her own sweater after trying to walk
in the footprint. "Ingratitude"
the name of our teenage dream.

But any Johnny's persistent knocking could wake us.
Jan and I couldn't see it through.
We stuck out in the crossed glamour and
only our names could fit into it. Kind of like cellophane.
My mother torn

between common sense and resentment.
Resolution praised her, curled the silver
and forced me to copy the family.
Johnny didn't approve.
My aunt came over, made a fuss.

We couldn't twiddle the feed-lot a day longer.
I shrugged off college, its promises "To be lived as a life."
Three grocery stores and a filling station put a damper
on dates and friendship. So fattening.
Mom offered cocoa (ready sign of forgiveness)

and the table skirt provided a suitable truce.
We worked hard on Jan's dress.
The sewing machine clacked Jan's secret
her hope dragged out.
In the closet a tangle of wire hangers swayed.

2.
Didn't know where we were going. "Train" meant nothing.
So we believed.
Nostalgia wasn't part of this. Jan's father
had tried out her speechlessness, her plans
were already single-file. (Johnny? Would I miss him?)

Laundry lines and dented trashcans went by.
Backyards were shabby poems. Chicago
was not a place yet. We were all bundles and knees.
Jan straightened her glasses. I never wrote
that poem—our special occasion, her freckles and reddish hair.

Ever Listening: Kristin Hersh

We drank silver hundred beers.
I'm crammed
thinking of drumheads
but instantly I grow plural.
Cologne whole constant, playing
"Gonna Shake Muscular Girl."
To hold you only, laughs a biker.

Guitar angles better, maybe his legs.
It's finally each spinning familiar
as Tea, Dave and I soon brake, though nothing stops.
Winter is the drummer, his last set loads out the cold.
We only wheeze coffee.
A time in we, when we were one-dollar funny
sounding part of no.

Guitar filling out easy against sound machines.
I need notes, the plunking just so. Of themselves
I say the meaning along the songs never. Don't thump
to shrieking and then suddenly tell it out worse.
Dreams shut time, tripping back sweet
but Tourette is songwriting my hair.
I of better seizure.

The Glads deliver the finish in sparkle mode.
Hovering in whiteness, hair stays
and the office steps back. Summer reinflates
fingers work, we'll meet you there.
Anyway, it was a payphone.
Call approximations
the screwed-up strings can still play what should've stuttered.

Angela Carter 1

Rode up on horseback
charging toward the vat
rescued herself
by plucking her plump
young form
from torture-mother's
glutinous blob of
chocolate pudding.

Nowadays she is the beatnik teen
practices Russian wrestling
stomach black from smoking.
Obscenities spew from the tips
of her winklepickers
letters kicking forth
word after word
the snapping kicks of typebars on a typewriter.

Protest Song

Kathleen Hanna:	You offered harm as a donation.
man:	Have I offended?
KH:	Ass slapper.
m:	All this yelling. You sick?
KH:	In a Lyme hospital bed with jello.
m:	The bedridden should act hopeful.
KH:	*Bitch* needs money.
m:	I give.

Heidi of the Alps

1.
Could climb it even now.
She suspected the sunlit mountain kept out-things out
no use fretting; the clock never whistled
had no meaning to a goat. In the pasture, a blue feather
she put in her hair the wind blew against a crag.
She would show them. Hens already knew.

She was mountainside. Little girls have strong feet.
Along the footpath the pungent morning air, goats.
The grass gave way to boulders chiseled by harried giants.
Peter yelled, "Far enough!"
Eyes on the jagged peaks beyond. Below them
wild rustling of firs. Paper bags and smokestacks.

2.
A poke from the horn. No need of a cup.
The moon opened and laughed.

3.
Goose dimpled arms in the cold
petticoat the color of the few floating flakes.
She imagined their mouths
as they watched her fall. But she flew back up
with a wriggling field mouse clenched in her beak.
She cocked her feathered little head
as she glanced down at them, pleased.

Fear Taught: Joan Rivers

1.
on your right
the dark thing
father's letter to a tramp
college strippers' dinner
you're not invited
crackers from the machine
get off stage
people expect
even from an amateur
one good thing
necklace from classmates
a climber fifth avenue
jab and punch
rarely real
corn-flaked motel
dirt-blackened tub
hard blinding
a foothold
the family can't hear it
your mother mink
father busting out
laughing at dinner
but can't interpret
his daughter
what will people think

2.
on your left
a man at a desk
ready patient smiling
recognizes you
something soft
the air unlocked
now the bank teller

she loves you
but tomorrow
if you arrive at the gate
and they don't let you in

Think About Something Else

They served us little flat fish,
the kind that enter the sky salted,

impassive, crunchy
amongst the clouds.

Sure, we were not used to flying,
wrote paragraphs with bullets.

But I knew which one was mine.
Big eyes in a little head.

The moms converge with a lesson:
Grandmas and cottage cheese.

You think that's poignant.
Vetch is forage for livestock.

"We're not livestock,"
eating tin beans, leaving our mothers

to pull the pins.
"Don't cry."

Johnny forgot his gun.
That's ok.

Memoir of Mary Gawthorpe, Suffragist

At the far end of a long dinner table
her story-lap
       hidden from us.
Polite descriptions, no portent.
She presents her father, but he
cannot be examined
a reverberating blur.
At bedtime, he
trespasses her bedroom
       she and her mother
his ungodly nightshirt, he waits
defiant, stubborn
demanding his wife.
An English summer with lilies he will wait.
And now we begin to see.
Mary stands up
       for her mother. *No!*
But we are at such a great distance.
We can't hear it.
       Will you tell us, Aunt Mary?
They say you were beaten.
You left that part out.
Heckling Churchill is dangerous.
But you knew that.

Tell us how
you arrived, *feminine little thing*
over becks
through ginnels, bumpy lanes.
Was it your mother's fine sewing
pointed the way?
Your older sister's Christmas tree angel
that informed your
       unimpetuous decisions?
Your paper route, little girl, heavy bag
or your tight-roping between

the men at the leather works.
And a whole chapter
listing *Whitaker's Almanacs* and *Yorkshire Posts*
strewn on couch and table.

It was the father you worked so hard—
painted the new walls yourself—
        to get the family away from.
His coming home at two in the morning
refusing your mother's questions.
Was it he who shaped you?

We don't know
you aren't famous enough.
Aunt Mary, how do soldiers talk?
How come you don't talk like one?
Tell me a story, Aunt Mary.

She Thinks They Still Remember: Jacqueline Jones

I wash collards, drain and shake thick stems
and coarsely chopped cabbage. Cover ham hocks
in cold water. Cooking for hours. Vinegar.

Kin clusters. The quilters are young, old, working.
Mothers on the couch: "Grandma or Hattie McDaniel?"

I stop moving the clothes a moment. Day-off get-togethers
in iron, hardly all of the wives, mothers. Outside is manly—
corn, bacon, molasses.

Seamstresses and hairdressers in the city's twilight.
Domestic service a scant vacation from hooking. History, stability, sanity,
humiliation. People with the right friends could help preserve your chin.

Or lodge with a genus you know nothing about. I feel cold
and noisy. Avoid the crowded rooms.
Now the house is quiet, dishes hot, table spread.
The ceiling fan makes the flower petals wave.
—Commotion of men and children.

Tell me the meaning of your blue ship-dress.

How many passengers can you capacitate?
Strong spaghetti straps provide safety

when ankles fail.
Too tight?

Your pumps are quite pumpy.
Me? I usually wear a three-piece boxcar

until my end starts.
I can't help it I always wear the same thing—

they counseled me on how to
regulate my paradoxes.

You guess I saw you floating. Yes I did, so?
Tell me the meaning of your glistening shoulders.

love tease blink   harass
Tell me.

Norma Jeane Mortenson

Butterfly bow shaped with
horsehair and ostrich feathers and wire.

The extra train
the halter neck laid flat against your chest

the pink gloves the black gloves
hidden hooks

$2.50 earrings sequin belt white fox stole
huge silk flowers

orphan clothes.

If i were naked i could be like the other girls.

Two old friends, hat
blue a feather.

Of '50
there was none around.

Popcorn falling
chair spring pokes.

"When will we see you?"

Riding sidesaddle weather monotonous
pomade so heavy.

Half buttons for nipples
skin-tight dahlia dress

skirt the censors.

Chiffon
single dropped jewel below the cleavage

the belt
the golden balls.

Radiating creases
   and sequins spiraling in every direction.

Not That Different: Angela Carter 2

Pink lace and steel-toe boots
  aren't worn inside.

If you're trying to segregate half
  the world's population
you're on your way.

III.

Thank you, next.

The girl pauses before exiting the stage.
The walls concave
a fault at the edge of her vision.
Everything happens then
but it's only one second.

Then the cracking plaster.
They stare at her
ignoring the chips
clicking as they bounce.
She doesn't move
listens to the guy's slow breathing
the bald one on the right

tapping his rolled-up script
on the seat back.
Only a second.
She never knows what happens next.
It's not a story.

Sadie

Light cannot find you
behind canned spinach and soap flakes,

the boxtops
shout merrily merrily.

Hide in the purse and smell
Wrigley's and powder, nervously

snapped open and closed
until your other has driven you home.

Sadie looking at you in the compact.

Down the hallway the study,
husband's ropey neck—quickstep!

Ah, now steam and bubbles are way up, fogging
your browline glasses. Drain the sink,

rather slide the dishes into slippery mineral oil,
curve of the bowl.

Your ear to the cat for the full throttle,
pillowy belly, warm.

Stroke the harlequin pillowcase, bells
on the corners, conjuring

this morning's sweater girl. Filene's hat counter.
What did you

want to whisper   soft?
Small enough to come inside your own pocketbook.

Calling Calling

She came naked to the bed, whispering
her name was Van Gogh.

I would've liked that, my beauty of her.
Mashed potatoes only came with garlic.

"Both of us!"
Only from thought I love I knew, remember.

Boode boode, we called out to each other
with a German *e*.

We looked slant into the miles,
saw each other's eyelashes.

The sunset was a place where a pool swimmer
spread his arms, "*So* beautiful."

It seems made up.
By midnight, peach cobbler

stuck to our teeth,
we swam in a circle.

Smell the love
cum and gravy.

Melva Kingman

Restless blue sweater mended, I wipe up
a pool of black ink. Nothing to consider.
Lorraine meets us
after school at Rexall's, gramophones in the store
earmuffs for listening. Haydn, Mozart—
the name of Elsie's street, but with a soft z.
Mom thinks we're seeing
Garbo in *The Painted Veil*,
but we sneak off to *Cleopatra* instead.
Tremendous wind walking home.

Tangerines in winter, my favorite.
Wake to cars buried in snow.
Peak inside the pages of music I can't read.
Beatrice from school has a piano at home
but we don't know her.
Dry cereal—the milkman must be stuck this morning.
Everything is hushed. Listen…
Pure white drifts, the sun plays it.
Imagine what's buried.
Snow riffs to the second story.

Marching: Sophia Duleep Singh

voice rattles
a high window
the lyric ricochets
then straightens
       to the upper register

breath comes
from the diaphragm
for the belters
on occasion
       the belly

trailing skirts out of fashion
wives sing wild
wrapped in bedsheets
to jump from a crawling baby
           is not a dance

talk of a women's parliament
words are for lemmings
feet do the work
until the pointlessness is stiff limbed
dogged bobbys
the street scuffle an avant-garde
               ballet

she fell down during the struggle
mud on her dress

"A Posterity Conceived and Born of Conscious Love"

god she said is not a baker
she knew very well the answer
say what you mean she was told
and she started here but went round the world
she told them she told them good
desperate the crowded house
would have it how long it took how far
to China for lunch Germany for chemicals
Ireland for drear she came back to a league
that wanted itself and needed themselves a waistline
she left for the clinic the clinic
lines to the corner crammed with how
with howling babies how many their ages
name address married or single
couldn't keep up she was thrown around
but kept her fingertips to herself felt the skin
tried to remember her father's face he said
the shape of the head reveals a person
and in the end she was the delicate of
a husband just the idea of it a comfort she was
dangling over space someone found her and helped her up
gave her a swat on the bottom sent her home
not a very long time something
not in mind yet something she would do
bending the knees can help follow these steps
will it be rhythm continence or pessaries jellies
and case histories and raids and the head
of the policewoman's bureau and husbands on the roof
the advancement of science civilized discoveries secrets
of life and all the while something so visible so obvious
just allow it just show them how is all

Viveka: Jarboe

No windows, heat or air conditioning
so you trust the group.
Group shuts you out
it's the new windows, heat, air conditioning.

Your black eyes fill with ice.
The swan. Not swans.
Your feather dips in a window
yet it doesn't get wet.

Girls Can't Lift Double: Liz Phair

Candy and stupid letters, bones.
Twelve jets in bed
    rocks, lightning.

Rough to stand shy in sunshine, kick me.
I rip weight off the door
        friends in flame.
    Rules, honey.

Wild egg in the basement.
Love business
        wounded thrill
    muffled twitch, tossed hat
        skip the stunts.

Press double: gatefold.
Alarm them:
    dollar falls *up* thru a hole in my pocket.

Now it's proven.
What to say after you say "told ya"?

Billie Holiday

Rat-a-matter faster
to drum up a compassion that he
did not know

those early senti-mellifluous bursts
such pretty snares.

Framer her
gardenia loop
tells the sing-song sing-along
first moment she to mother
                        maid in Baltimore.

Be close to a man and did everything she could to stop her.

This must have been
in the middle of May.

Dolly

"Goose *can* negotiate?"
The game's a hustle.
Poor old 'mucks thought
they could chisel her.
With her remainder
she mails kids forests
anthropomorphized bears.

Élisabeth Louise Vigée Le Brun & Amy Schumer

1. <u>Vigée Le Brun</u>
Self-Portrait with Cerise Ribbons, ca. 1782
Self-Portrait with Her Daughter Julie, 1786

where's the point
   of shine
a delicate nose
not serious
   they say
of direction
do they not undertake
   to pin a craft
their work adornment
   a self-promotion they say
so it must be her face
   its fineness they doubt

light the face
   night
color the neck
   and shadow
no broken tooth
   brittle ends
but soft curls
   on muslin shoulders
scarves interlace
   ribbons
slightly part her lips

"her maternity"
   smiles the canvas
no reason
   to become weary

2. Schumer
Vogue, July 2016
Photographer: Annie Leibovitz
Makeup: Gucci Westman
Dress: Naeem Khan

others volumize her hair
   pack her body
she knows to perform
   walk here
lift the dress
the generous
   red flowered
fabric should not
   drag the pavement

she wants a gag
they allow her a scone
   with cloth napkin

Plural: Kembra Pfahler

Beige heels she kicks off
clatter the hardwood.
"My menopausal body"
she tells the camera

unbuttoning her shirt.
The filmmakers assume she's making excuses.
But they never explain the phrase:
"your true self."

She slips off her pants
takes her seat
on the high stool
puts on a proud face.

Margaret Cho

It takes a lot of hours to study a studied woman.

Her face is round.
Mine is long and narrow.

References

1   "How Did It Make You Feel When They Found You" is based on *Lulu in Hollywood* by silent film star Louise Brooks.

2   "Matriarch" is influenced by *Dancing Fish and Ammonites* by Penelope Lively.

3   "Lost Objects" is influenced by *M Train* by Patti Smith.

4   "The Way Back Home" is a fictional poem that uses *Curriculum Vitae* by Muriel Spark as a starting point.

6   "Josephine Marcus Earp" is based on *Lady at the O.K. Corral: The True Story of Josephine Marcus Earp* by Ann Kirschner.

7   "Clarice Lispector" is based on her life by way of *Why This World: A Biography of Clarice Lispector* by Benjamin Moser. The poem is also influenced by *Near to the Wild Heart* by Clarice Lispector.

8   "Help Me Out Can You" is based on the lives of Elizabeth Holloway Marston, Olive Byrne, and William Moulton Marston by way of *The Secret History of Wonder Woman* by Jill Lepore.

9   "Cherie Currie" is based on *Neon Angel: A Memoir of a Runaway* by Cherie Currie.

11   "Garbo/Dietrich" is based on pertinent sections of *The Girls: Sappho Goes to Hollywood* by Diana McLellan.

12   "Sure: Mother Maybelle" draws upon sections of *Cash* by Johnny Cash where he describes his mother-in-law, Maybelle Carter.

14   "H.D., the Book" draws upon *The H.D. Book* by Robert Duncan and borrows from the poem "Heat" by H.D. ("plough through ... on either side")

17   "Covered" is influenced by *Barefoot in Baghdad: A Story of Identity— My Own and What It Means to Be a Woman in Chaos* by Manal Omar.

20   "Leaving Home, 1959" borrows characters and situations from *The Girls in 3-B* by Valerie Taylor.

22   "Ever Listening" is influenced by *Rat Girl: A Memoir* by Kristin Hersh.

23   "Angela Carter 1" is based on *The Invention of Angela Carter* by Edmund Gordon.

24   The line "The bedridden should act hopeful" comes from a comment Kathleen Hanna made to the audience at a The Julie Ruin concert at the Fillmore Auditorium, San Francisco, November 1, 2014.

25   "Heidi of the Alps" borrows characters and situations from *Heidi* by Johanna Spyri.

26   "Fear Taught" is based on *Enter Talking* by Joan Rivers.

29   "Memoir of Mary Gawthorpe, Suffragist" is a reaction to *Up Hill to Holloway* by Mary Gawthorpe, the great-grandaunt of the poet's wife.

31   "She Thinks They Still Remember" is influenced by *Labor of Love, Labor of Sorrow: Black Women, Work, and the Family, from Slavery to the Present* by Jacqueline Jones.

33   "Norma Jeane Mortenson" borrows clothing items from *Dressing Marilyn: How a Hollywood Icon was Styled by William Travilla* by Andrew Hansford and Karen Homer.

39   "Thank you, next." is based on an anecdote from Joyce Carol Oates during an interview at the San Francisco Jewish Community Center, May 2007.

43   "Marching" uses biographical information about Sophia Duleep Singh from *Sophia: Princess, Suffragette, Revolutionary* by Anita Anand.

44   "'A Posterity Conceived and Born of Conscious Love'" is based on the life of Margaret Sanger by way of *Margaret Sanger: An Autobiography*. The title is a quote from her book.

45   "Viveka: Jarboe" is based on a Jarboe interview found on YouTube, underyourskindvd channel.

46   "Girls Can't Lift Double: Liz Phair" borrows from the albums *Exile in Guyville* by Liz Phair and *Exile on Main Street* by The Rolling Stones.

47   "Billie Holiday" is influenced by *With Billie* by Julia Blackburn.

51   "Plural" is based on a YouTube video of Kembra Pfahler, StyleLikeU channel.

53   "Margaret Cho" is influenced by *I Have Chosen to Stay and Fight* by Margaret Cho, and her concert film *I'm the One That I Want,* and the website margaretcho.com.

Thank you to Rusty Morrison for her invaluable feedback as I worked to complete this book.

Thank you to all the workshop participants and poetry groupmates who helped me along the way.

Thank you to my wife, Katy Miessner, for the artwork and to Krystal Hipps for the cover.

Special thanks to Rebecca Stoddard for helping me get started in the world of poetry eleven years ago.

Jeffrey Kingman lives by the Napa River in Vallejo, California. He has written several books, including the chapbook, *On a Road*, which was published by Finishing Line Press in 2019. *Beyond That Hill I Gather*, won the 2018 Eyelands Book Award (Greece) for an unpublished poetry book. He also wrote a young adult novel, *Moto Girl* (unpublished), about a 12-year-old girl learning to ride motocross.

Jeff is the winner of the 2012 *Revolution House* Flash Fiction Contest, and the winner of the Red Berry Editions 2015 Broadside Contest. He has been a finalist in many contests including the 2018 Hillary Gravendyk Prize poetry book competition, the 2015 Blue Light Press Chapbook Competition, the 2014 Sow's Ear Poetry Competition, and the 2013 Frost Place Chapbook Fellowship. He has been published in *PANK, Crack the Spine, Squaw Valley Review, The Offbeat, Sparkle & Blink, lo-ball, Off Channel, Grey Sparrow, decomP, North Atlantic Review, Picaroon Poetry, Visitant* and others.

Jeff has a Master's degree in Music Composition and has played drums in rock bands most of his life.

www.ingramcontent.com/pod-product-compliance
Lightning Source LLC
Chambersburg PA
CBHW021201090426
42740CB00008B/1183